Notes for Echo Lake

Michael Palmer

North Point Press
San Francisco

Copyright © 1981 by Michael Palmer
Printed in the United States of America

LIBRARY OF CONGRESS
CATALOGING-IN-PUBLICATION DATA
Palmer, Michael, 1943–
Notes for Echo Lake.

I. Title.
PS3566.A54N6   811'.54   80-28436
ISBN 0-86547-024-3

SECOND PRINTING

North Point Press
850 Talbot Avenue
Berkeley, California
94706

for Clark Coolidge

Contents

"Place there is none; we go forward and backward
and there is no place . . ."
Augustine, *Confessions,* X.25-6

"Big Sid Catlett Art Tatum Fats Navarro"
Helmut Heissenbüttel, 'Topographies'

The Comet

"An outlook based upon philosophy became obligatory."
Bruno Schulz

That year the end of winter stood under a sign
All days were red in the margin
writ large against the ochre rooftops
                          and yes that was your father's

face, a murder best forgotten
by passersby inured to the dust
though blinded a bit by the redness
                          Invisible charges rose

in the poles, only
to enclose them, a parody of juggling
within the lap of eternal matter
                    like love c. mid-afternoon

eyes half-open, adjustments
at an unexpected point of the experiment
occurred toward the backstage of things
                                    warm

currents of air and some really
depressing tricks that filled one
with true melancholy
                    regarding *principium individuationis*

suitable more to the success of an idea
in an illustrated journal
of modern physics
                    splendidly bogus

and immediately satisfying
as forecast long ago by the prophets
in a circus farce

Notes for Echo Lake   1

"I am glad to see you Ion."

He says this red as dust, eyes a literal self among selves and picks the coffee up.

Memory is kind, a kindness, a kind of unlistening, a grey wall even toward which you move.

It was the woman beside him who remarked that he never looked anyone in the eye. (This by water's edge.)

This by water's edge.

And all of the song 'divided into silences', or 'quartered in three silences'.

Dear Charles, I began again and again to work, always with no confidence as Melville might explain. Might complain.

A message possibly intercepted, possibly never written. A letter she had sent him.

But what had his phrase been exactly, "Welcome to the Valley of Tears," or maybe "Valley of Sorrows." At least one did feel welcome, wherever it was.

A kind of straight grey wall beside which they walk, she the older by a dozen years, he carefully unlistening.

Such as words are. A tape for example a friend had assembled containing readings by H.D., Stein, Williams, others. Then crossing the bridge to visit Zukofsky, snow lightly falling.

Breaking like glass Tom had said and the woman from the island. Regaining consciousness he saw first stars then a face leaning over him and heard the concerned voice, "Hey baby you almost got *too* high."

Was was and is. In the story the subject disappears.

They had agreed that the sign was particular precisely because arbitrary and that it included the potential for (carried the sign of) its own dissolution, and that there was a micro-syntax below the order of the sentence and even of the word, and that in the story the subject disappears it never disappears. 1963: only one of the two had the gift of memory.

Equally one could think of a larger syntax, e.g. the word-as-book proposing always the book-as-word. And of course still larger.

Beginning and ending. As a work begins and ends itself or begins and rebegins or starts and stops. Ideas as elements of the working not as propositions of a work, even in a propositional art. (Someone said someone thought.)

That is, snow
        a) is
        b) is not
                falling – check neither or both.

If one lives in it. 'Local' and 'specific' and so on finally seeming less interesting than the 'particular' wherever that may locate.

"What I really want to show here is that it is not at all clear *a priori* which are the simple colour concepts."

Sign that empties itself at each instance of meaning, and how else to reinvent attention.

Sign that empties . . . That is *he* would ask *her*. He would be the asker and she unlistening, nameless mountains in the background partly hidden by cloud.

The dust of course might equally be grey, the wall red, our memories perfectly accurate. A forest empty of trees, city with no streets, a man having swallowed his tongue. As there is no 'structure' to the sentence and no boundary or edge to the field in question. As there is every-where no language.

As I began again and again, and each beginning identical with the next, meaning each one accurate, each a projection, each a head bending over the motionless form.

And he sees himself now as the one motionless on the ground, now as the one bending over. Lying in an alley between a house and a fence (space barely wide enough for a body), opening his eyes he saw stars and heard white noise followed in time by a face and a single voice.

Now rain is falling against the south side of the house but not the north where she stands before a mirror.

"Don't worry about it, he's already dead."

"Te dérange pas, il est déjà mort."

"È morto lei, non ti disturba."

She stands before the mirror touches the floor. Language reaches for the talk as someone falls. A dead language opens and opens one door.

So here is color. Here is a color darkening or color here is a darkening. Here white remains . . .

And you indicate the iris of the portrait's eye, a specific point on the iris, wanting that colour as your own. There is a grey wall past which we walk arm in arm, fools if we do greater fools if we don't.

And I paint the view from my left eye, from the balcony of the eye overlooking a body of water, an inland sea possibly, possibly a man-made lake.

And do I continue as the light changes and fades, eventually painting in pitch dark. That is, if you write it has it happened twice:

> It rained again that night deep inside
> where only recently had occurred the abandonment of signs

Portrait Now Before Then

That is A, that is Anna speaking. That is A, that is no one speaking and it's winter. That is a bridge and a bridge of winter pure as talk.

The river is red.

I'm offering a name.

The river begins between sheer cliffs. There are parts of words in it.

What he heard was winter talking.

I'm erasing one name.

Here is A in a story of first things, things first seen as they were speaking, fire before water and a sun that's one foot wide.

That is A crossing a bridge and a letter is that which it says it is. One A means winter. Casey Daedalus survived the war.

* * *

In his dream the bell rings and rings until she wakes to a perfect copy of herself as a polished stone falling from a lighted window toward the welcoming arms of the crowd below.

In his dream the robed and bearded men stand beneath the letter-tree. I hold out my left arm and read the word 'cloud' as it appears there. She shows me the tiny butterfly painted on the back of her hand. By then we have become the four weeping men.

* * *

In the *Comprehensive Treatise on Naked Skin* he reads that the occasional dark spots are not blemishes but characteristic features of the Victorian glaze.

The light narrows to a light above a door and the world grows, briefly, cold. Reading the eyes glaze, a bell summons winter from our sleep.

We stumbled over shards of rose-quartz across hills where nothing remained, hills where nothing had been left. We visit those hills from which.

In his dream he sees himself as a name, hears an identical name and recalls four words each day. In A's dream a crowd is whispering.

* * *

What do the letters spell.

Once he walked on the frozen common and once a dog found him.

Probing the heart for ways of grace, yellow, purple and white flowering on the same stalk.

And once he lay face down in snow and that became the dream.

What do the letters mean.

An A is an ending in full sun, another resembles its shadow, and the third is that which it says it is. They entered tired and wet.

As each wheel of meeting turns in a wheel, each letter is spoken to begin. For an entire year the river was dry, but the following spring it poured through the streets.

He wondered about the terms, what they called 'parts of speech', and the words one couldn't say. Everything had what was known as 'its place'.

House of mud or house of stone and the crowd with outstretched arms. At dawn gulls gather on rooftops. Things try to stand for other things. I'm coming to the age I am.

False Portrait of Hanna H

Empty faces of
and tomorrow's alternate idea
announced in careful white letters

which cover a hillside
and spell nothing
Out of boredom apparently

she had drowned him in the muddy water
then abandoned the clothes beneath a nearby tree
the endless halls unexpectedly full

so that it becomes almost impossible to leave
I only remember the mountain
traced again and again with a blue brush

and seeming finally to float
beyond the plain of violet, ochre and green
and the unfinished house

at a turning in the road
and the sharpness of the rock
arms raised behind her head

or the sudden sharpness of the rock
and the rider's grey horse
before the city walls

Notes for Echo Lake 2

He would assume a seeing into the word, whoever was there to look.
Would care to look. A coming and going in smoke.

A part and apart.

Voices through a wall. They are there because we hear them what do we
hear. The pitch rises toward the end to indicate a question.

What's growing in the garden.

To be at a loss for words. How does the mind move there, walking
beside the bank of what had been a river. How does the light.

And rhythm as an arm, rhythm as the arm extended, he turns and turns
remembering the song. What did she recall.

It was of course the present the sibyl most clearly saw, reading the
literal signs, the words around her, until a further set of signs appeared.
And to divine the fullness of the message she uttered would demand of
her listener an equivalent attention. The message was the world trans-
lated, and speaker and listener became one. Her message was the sign
itself.

Hermes alike as the bearer and concealer. Hermes as the sign.

Who lives in the speaking and unlistening, wild onions by the river, roses in the garden a hundred years old, lilac, iris, poppy, jasmine trellised above the kitchen window.

They walk beside departure and images of a dry riverbed unfold, voices through a wall arm in arm. They walk beside an answer typing each letter as it appears. A large white room has a beamed ceiling. The poor live in long rows.

While staring at the sea he paints a woman's face, requests more light and time. Is there ever an image that appears, word inside word, skin blue as dust, nameless hills beyond. Is there an image if there is.

To be at a loss and to return there, saying things and speaking, it's started to rain. He paints a woman's face the color of the sea but portrays someone else as an empty chair. Then he learns to erase four words each day.

As an arm folded might mean 'to flow'.

They collide near the cafe door, smile politely and pass. He watches the philosopher turn the corner and disappear.

There is agreeable poetry.

There is poetry like a white cloth.

There's a poetry licking its tongue.

Let me lend you my fork.

Voice occurs through a wall.

As song divides itself, she explains with a wave.

We have never been happy here have never been happier.

November Talks

for Bob Perelman

Certain faces seem to be ours
pieces of April broken from the main part
window and door entirely ours
who dream of the path of ice
beneath shade, sleep flowering

casually over narrow shoulders
and wheels of a given day within wheels
A headless man is crossing the road
as we remember the earliest shore
outlined by cloud, sleep

wet to our touch, material
of tears offered in sips
so many of us
here, so many missing
who might have been here

A Dream Called 'The House of Jews'

for J.R. & D.R.

Many gathered many friends maybe everyone
Many now and then may have entered
The ivory teeth fell from her mouth
The typewriter keys
Many fell then at the entrance
Many held them
Many fell forward and aware
Various friends gathered at the entrance
Some held back
The room contains a question
Many said now before then this then that
The room contains a question to be named
He said *I will tell the book the dream the words tell me*
The room is not the place or the name

Notes for Echo Lake   3

Words that come in smoke and go.

Some things he kept, some he kept and lost. He loved the French poets
fell through the partly open door.

And I as it is, I as the one but less than one in it. I was the blue against
red and a voice that emptied, and I is that one with broken back.

While April is ours and dark, as something always stands for
what is: dying elm, headless man, winter –

salamander, chrysalis,

fire –

grammar and silence.

Or grammar against silence. Years later they found themselves talking
in a crowd. Her white cat had been killed in the woods behind her
house. It had been a good possibly even a terrible winter. Ice had coated
the limbs of the hawthorn and lilac, lovely but dangerous. Travel plans
had been made then of necessity abandoned. At different times entire
weeks had seemed to disappear. She wondered what initially they had
agreed not to discuss.

Some things he kept while some he kept apart.

As Robert's call on Tuesday asking whether I knew that Zukofsky had died a couple of days before. The call came as I was reading a copy of Larry Rivers' talk at Frank O'Hara's funeral (July, 1966), "He was a quarter larger than usual. Every few inches there was some sewing composed of dark blue thread. Some stitching was straight and three or four inches long, others were longer and semi-circular . . ."

As Robert's call on Tuesday a quarter larger than usual asking whether I knew whether I knew. Blue thread every few inches, straight and semi-circular, and sand and wet snow. Blue snow a couple of days before. Whether I know whatever I know.

The letters of the words of our legs and arms. What he had seen or thought he'd seen within the eye, voices overheard rising and falling. And if each conversation has no end, then composition is a placing beside or with and is endless, broken threads of cloud driven from the west by afternoon wind.

The letters of the words of our legs and arms. In the garden he dreamt he saw four bearded men and listened to them discussing metaphor. They are standing at the points of the compass. They are standing at the points of the compass and saying nothing. They are sitting in the shade of a flowering tree. She is holding the child's body out toward the camera. She is standing before the mirror and asking. She is offering and asking. He-she is asking me a question I can't quite hear. Evenings they would walk along the shore of the lake.

Letters of the world. Bright orange poppy next to white rose next to blue spike of larkspur and so on. Artichoke crowding garlic and sage. Hyssop, marjoram, orange mint, winter and summer savory, oregano, trailing rosemary, fuchsia, Dutch iris, day lily, lamb's tongue, lamb's ears, blackberry, feverfew, lemon verbena, sorrel, costmary, never reads it as it is, "poet living tomb of his/games."

Eyes eyeing what self never there, as things in metaphor cross, are
thrown across, a path he calls the path of names. In the
film *La Jetée* she is thrown against time and is marking time:

> sun burns thru the roars
> dear eyes, *all eyes,* pageant
> bay inlet, garden casuarina, spittle-spawn
> (not laurel) nameless we name
> it, and sorrows dissolve – human

In silence he would mark time listening for whispered words. I began
this in spring, head ready to burst, flowers, reddening sky, moon with a
lobster, New York, Boston, return, thin coating of ice, moon while
dogs bark, moon dogs bark at, now it's late fall.

And now he told me it's time to talk.

Words would come in smoke and go, inventing the letters of the
voyage, would walk through melting snow to the corner store for
cigarettes, oranges and a newspaper, returning by a different route past
red brick townhouses built at the end of the Civil War. Or was the
question in the letters themselves, in how by chance the words were
spelled.

In the poem he learns to turn and turn, and prose seems always
a sentence long.

False Portrait of D.B. as Niccolò Paganini

Those who have lived here since before
time are gone while the ones who must
replace them have not yet arrived.

The streets are wet with a recent
rain yet you continue to count
first minutes and hours then trees

rocks, windows, mailboxes, streetlights
and pictographs refusing to
rest even for the brief span it

would take to dry off, change clothes and
reemerge grotesque yet oddly
attractive like Paganini

whose mother was visited by
a seraph in Genoa not
long before his birth and who is

thought now to have acquired much of
his technical wizardry as
a result of Marfan's syndrome

a quite common anomaly
of the connective tissues which
may well account for the tall and

angular body, muscular
underdevelopment as well
as the hypermobile joints that

eventuated on the stage
in a peculiar stance, a
spectacular bowing technique

and an awesome mastery of
the fingerboard. He would bring his
left hip forward to support his

body's weight. His left shoulder, thrust
forward also, would enable
him to rest his left elbow on

his chest, a buttress against the
stress of forceful bowing along
with debilitating muscle

fatigue. The looseness of the right
wrist and shoulder gave pliancy
leading to broad acrobatic

bowing. The 'spider' fingers of
his left hand permitted a range
on the fingerboard which many

attributed to black magic
for Paganini was said to
have signed a pact with Lucifer

to acquire virtuosity
as a small child. After his death
perhaps due in part to this tale

in part also to rumours of
gambling and wild debauchery
the Church refused to allow him

burial on hallowed ground. In
consequence his body was moved
furtively from place to place

until after many years and
for reasons still mysterious
the Church finally relented.

A few paradoxes should be
noted as an afterword. Though
accused of charlatanism he

was rewarded for his skill like
no one before him. He loved his
violin above all yet once

he gambled it away at cards.
He accepted wealth and renown
from his worshipping admirers

but tripled the admission price
to his concerts in the face of
adverse reviews. While openly

irreverent of tradition
he still took a princess as his lover
and let nations strike medals in his name.

To Robert E. Symmes 1933
for a gift of resemblances

His arm slept. Dream-wounded and a former
figure he wept beside the stream
to see himself becoming it.
Who would write him in as a target
burned by the sun
who heard a name he would become
or once was, red
as a second following dawn? The city
is full of ones called us
who endlessly greet each other by a name
that changes each time.
It's a wonder to return, head aching,
to witness the bear to its rest
and it's odd to wake and rewrite it
as a kind of resemblance.
I am tired and would like to leave.
I have never been here. The book
wears a lion's mane. For a moment
they were visitors resembling themselves.
Laughing he had said, I am tired of this waiting to be born.
The ones called figures crowd the street.
Each is missing part of his name
and each longs to be drawn a face.

11 v 79

Notes for Echo Lake   4

Who did he talk to

Did she trust what she saw

Who does the talking

Whose words formed awkward curves

Did the lion finally talk

Did the sleeping lion talk

Did you trust a north window

What made the dog bark

What causes a grey dog to bark

What does the juggler tell us

What does the juggler's redness tell us

Is she standing in an image

Were they lost in the forest

Were they walking through a forest

Has anything been forgotten

Did you find it in the dark

Is that one of them new atomic-powered wristwatches

Was it called a talking song

Is that an oblong poem

Was poetry the object

Was there once a road here ending at a door

Thus from bridge to bridge we came along

Did the machine seem to talk

Did he read from an empty book

Did the book grow empty in the dark, grey felt hat blowing down the
street, arms pumping back and forth, legs slightly bowed

Are there fewer ears than songs

Did he trust a broken window

Did he wake beneath a tree in the recent snow

Whose words formed difficult curves

Have the exaggerations quieted down

The light is lovely on trees which are not large

23

My logic is all in the melting-pot

My life now is very economical

I can say nothing of my feeling about space

Nothing could be clearer than what you see on this wall

Must we give each one a name

Is it true they all have names

Would it not have been simpler

Would it not have been simpler to begin

Were there ever such buildings

I must remember to mention the trees

I must remember to invent some trees

Who told you these things

Who taught you how to speak

Who taught you not to speak

Whose is the voice that empties

A book of

A book of nothing gives
him its elbow
or its fist.
Palms followed by wind
carrying salt. Grey dogs
at the edge of the road.
It's time to walk and walk
pretending to be lost.
Look straight up
at the creased rock
the color of a tongue.
The rest
seemed to be metal.
You will write some salt.

So with his daughter Antigone

So with his daughter Antigone
passing the slow days in Vienna
aware of the warm spots on the body
danger recumbent as a cloud
against an arm, head raised in
gesture of greeting or farewell
legs planted slightly apart
aware of the warm spots beyond the body
arms extended to signify welcome
present world defined as standing for itself
enter here if you walk backward there if too fast
a succession of stones we are made of
pale *region where the light is bent*
has come to resemble not exactly a mountain

Through Time

You are in for another surprise too
"Good-by Bess" – chasm
cutting away to the left – a world
curved above the green water
hummingbird with violet-banded neck
so many brinks
to balance and inspire
say, a Victorian haberdasher
relaxed and confident
creature I would perhaps not altogether trust
waddling up
no larger than a child's coffin
suspended at eye-level
waiting for the life to start

Notes for Echo Lake   5

"a blue under people"
Bernadette Mayer, *Memory*

The tree's green explains what a light means, an idea, the bomb or
Donald Duck, a box of marbles in a marble box, the amber jewel
behind the toad's eyes reminds us that it's night. The interpreter of the
text examines the traffic light, coughs and lays the book aside. The dead
mayor sits behind his desk, overcome with wonderment.

The interpreter of a cough examines the light and lays the text aside.
Here and there leaves, clouds, rivers of tears in the streets meant a sonata
for tongues.

Truth to tell the inventor of the code weeps and lays the text aside. Here
and there calendars and walls remind him that it's night, a sleeping lion
is curled up in one corner, a voice can be heard behind a door, and Plato
told us of the law, Plato warned us about the poem. The dead mayor
wonders if the King of France is bald.

Today is an apparent day of empty sleeves and parallelograms, and red
meaning red, and the flag as an object, and red instead of red, the flag as
an object with undulating sides, the spider who taught me to walk, the
emptiness of the code, the spider who forgot how to walk, the delicate
curves within the code, three barking dogs, the mystery of intervals, the
absence of a code, the lion asleep at her feet, the empty sleeve waving,
the bottle now broken, the voices she told him to listen for, the stolen
book, the measurement of intervals.

Does physics know Caesar by name?

Plato warned us of the shadows of the poem, of the words cast against the wall, and Plato warns against the song.

The tree's green explains what a name means apart from memory, flickers of light in the darkened room, our eyes fixed on the screen on the figures of nothing.

The inventor of the code hears each note and swallows his tongue, frightened by shadows. The lion red as a lobster is green sleeps in one corner dreaming of the hours' numbers and names, a river flowing at his feet. "Shuffle Montgomery" was the song.

And here and there they speak in tongues, correcting the right notes in order to get them wrong. And how many days did you spend underground?

The interpreter of leaves examines each tear as pages turn. In the field at dawn they cross swords and a head rolls while the audience laughs. The dead city listens to the code as it reads, and a poem moves back and forth.

At our feet like a sky the graceful curve. Rumours that they are lovers or were in a previous lifetime made of salt. Hills beyond tipped with snow or salt, a curve broken off, searching for her tongue. A deep blue tasting of salt. The awkward curve and talking cloud, steps toward a forest for want of stairs. Are in a lifetime or were. Rumours that the sender had forgotten the code and swallowed his tongue. A mirror in one corner was about to fall, apparently his memory of Siena and the dome.

And Brother Mouse with parachute in mid-air, forever descending.

That they are figures or were, a pictograph with thumb extended. He drank from an actual glass of beer. An outstretched arm offers me its hand.

Song of the Round Man

for Sarah when she's older

The round and sad-eyed man puffed cigars as if
he were alive. Gillyflowers
to the left of the apple, purple bells to the right

and a grass-covered hill behind.
I am sad today said the sad-eyed man
for I have locked my head in a Japanese box

and lost the key.
I am sad today he told me
for there are gillyflowers by the apple

and purple bells I cannot see.
Will you look at them for me
he asked, and tell me what you find?

I cannot I replied
for my eyes have grown sugary and dim
from reading too long by candlelight.

Tell me what you've read then
said the round and sad-eyed man.
I cannot I replied

for my memory has grown tired and dim
from looking at things that can't be seen
by any kind of light

and I've locked my head in a Japanese box
and thrown away the key.
Then I am you and you are me

said the sad-eyed man as if alive.
I'll write you in where I should be
between the gillyflowers and the purple bells

and the apple and the hill
and we'll puff cigars from noon till night
as if we were alive.

Seven Forbidden Words

"Mon chat sur le carreau cherchant une litière"
Baudelaire, 'Spleen'

Who peered from the invisible world
toward a perfectly level field. Terms
will be broken here (have been broken here).
Should a city of blue tile appear
no one will be listening there.
He stood up, walked across the room
and broke his nose against the door.
A was the face of a letter
reflected in the water below.
He watched cross-eyed
learning a few words at a time.
The sun rose behind your shoulder
and told me to act casual
while striking an attitude of studied repose.
You grew these flowers yourself
so how could you forget their names.
The yellow one is said to be uncommon
and the heart tastes as expected, tender
and bitter like an olive
but less violent. It has been summer for a day
or part of a day
with shades drawn. The fires were deliberately set
and the inhabitants welcomed them.

The Flower of Capital

(sermon faux – vraie histoire)

> "Not as a gesture of contempt for the scattered nature of reality."
> Spicer, *The Heads of the Town Up to the Aether*

The flower of capital is small and white large and grey-green in a storm its petals sing. (This refers to capital with the capital *L*.) Yesterday I borrowed Picabia's Lagonda for a drive through the Bois. A heavy mist enveloped the park so that we could barely discern the outline of a few silent figures making their way among the sycamores and elms. Emerging at Porte de Neuilly the air grew suddenly clear and ahead to my right I noticed M pushing a perambulator before her with a distracted mien. Her hair fell disheveled about her face, her clothes were threadbare, and every few steps she would pause briefly and look about as if uncertain where she was. I tried repeatedly to draw her attention with the horn, even slowing down at one point and crying her name out the car window, all to no apparent effect. Passing I saw once more (and as it developed, for the last time) the lenticular mark on her forehead and explained its curious origin to my companion, the Princess von K, who in return favored me with her wan smile. We drove on directly to the Château de Verre where the Princess lived with her younger sister and a few aged servants. The château itself was encircled by the vestiges of a moat now indicated only by a slight depression in the grass at the base of the walls. Or: we drove for hours through the small towns surrounding Paris, unable to decide among various courses of action. Or: they have unearthed another child's body bringing the current total to twenty-eight. Or: nine days from now will occur the vernal equinox. Yesterday in the artificial light of a large hall Ron spoke to me of character hovering unacceptably at several removes above the page. The image of the Princess and of M who were of course one and the same returned to mind as I congratulated him on the accuracy of his observation. L knitted this shirt I told him, and carved the sign on my brow, and only yesterday they removed the tree that for so long had interfered with the ordered flow of language down our street. Capital is a fever at play and in the world (silent *l*) each thing is real or must pretend to be. Her tongue swells until it fills my mouth. I have lived here for a day or part of a day, eyes closed, arms hanging casually at my sides. Can such a book be read by you or me? Now he lowers the bamboo shade to alter the angle of the light, and now she breaks a fingernail against the railing of the bridge. Can such a text invent its own beginning, as for example: one – two – three? And can it curve into closure from there to here?

Notes for Echo Lake   6

A tree's streaming imitates light. Water gathers light behind the arm. The arm is 'held' there. Water bodies light to divide. Light measures by resemblance. Water filters bridge as in left-handedness. Light alters it. Water patterns bridge against its step. Hills cancel redness. Body empties and divides. Body's shift patterns bridge this river is called. Here trees cancel bodies light sometimes marks. An angle occurs in selection. Here trees are marks. Here trees begin a cancelled pattern. He sometimes hears them. Coffee is sent. Here dancing is done in fear across rooftops.

Documentation

"This is how it happened"
                    Homeric Hymn to Demeter

This road ends in a field of grain
and drunken crows are filling the air
or how do we know what we know

He spoke holding his severed ear
The sky moves too quickly through the frame
and the smile has been put on sideways

Veiled Hecate lives in three bodies
lit by approximate light
The daughter receives grief and is alive

The daughter recites grief and is alive
as the mother places her in the fire
and the child holds her yellow hair out

wondering why it's been cut
The bearded tree is the third part
where the ages of the barley hang down

They have loved a secret architecture
that leaves false evidence of itself
and they love to be as three in one

Our visit has lasted an entire winter
and we have half forgotten each word's name
The sky moves that quickly through the frame

False Portrait

(of H. as N.)

He-she bends at the mirrored waist
is seen is visible to a given face
who drowned in the myth of a three crossing four

Twice we died in the great frog war
you me and Henry with his hand
Henry with his hand against the page
wondering what not what never to draw

He is growing red rings around his eyes
Our own recent photographs of those planets show
far greater detail than ever before

He-she gazes at the face in the water
Jason hopes to find something there
Any number of coughs are calling
The water's body has stored up light

Pre-Petrarchan Sonnet

(after Peter Altenberg)

Someone identical with Dante
sits beside a stone. Enough
is enough is enough of.
It's odd that your hand feels warm
(snow carefully falling).
It's odd that the page was torn
just where the snow had begun.
There was never very much.
There is more (less) than there was.
Today it is 84, 74 and 12
and light and dark.
We are nowhere else.
His smile fell to one side.
Here and there it was very light and dark.

Notes for Echo Lake   7

So this was the story is a story gibbous moon 1:10 AM he falls toward
the world from a bridge yes god made me not a tooth in my head what
next grey dog barks while sphere inside sphere rusts beside the fence
god unnamed me in a snit but I woke up then left arm bent behind my
back clear sky overhead so this is this and fireflies are a part of it crickets
white spiders remnants of the cedar forest in which he hid rain fee fie
falling then chemical sun then rain again meaning winter remnants of
the forest in which he'd lived miniscule yellow flower streaked with blue
tiny fingers and wrists figures star-crossed at the mid-point words and
blood commingling leaves not green but dull and dark boughs twisted
and gnarled we climbed to a hilltop obscured by mist sat and talked
nothing more muffled concussion of guns a few miles off gentle breeze
scented with rosemary and sage grey dog barks at a rock fell from a
high place while reading a circular book Chinese dream rusting against
the fence sphere within sphere within sphere the limit is three one now
one then one what or when hair and eyes considered simply as elements
of the composition day we assumed would follow day one you one me
one he-she-it muddy stream below a window wharf rats at play in arc-
light one nod of noggin and one Mincka Mauss landscape in which
figures rarely appear golondrina golonfina and the rest *here lies Howard*
Fink his words were blue and his undies pink sparrow hawk barely larger
than your palm sign that empties sitting and talking nothing more fell
toward the world itself right arm extended to protect his face grey dog
barking at the clock shattering of glass beyond the courtyard wall
followed by laughter myself we saw passing with eyes shaded against

the glare lover with gryphon's wings kneeling in an attitude of prayer waves lapping at the foot of our bed have been had been ill somewhat ill three suns crossing a winter sky myself in blue velvet jacket strolling past the half-open window ghost following one holds a lamp the other a sword and a sponge blue as of mountains rust broken words after language wide toothless grin open words after language blue as of a greeting or sudden end one mark indicating what blue as of a letter red as of a name written backward.

Seven Lines of Equal Length

"Simplement parole et geste."
Mallarmé, *Igitur*

1

He describes a city that apparently never was
thus the sun bending
and the paperback's blue spine
telling of a voyage
past memory into a copse or grove fitted with doors
The sun is an artificial one
and he has lost three-hundred pounds
by listening to Chopin in the background
the Nocturnes and Preludes by day
and the Gizmos by artificial night
so deceptively simple to play

This letter will never reach you
and as long as we both know it's ok
Did the other one reach you
and if so what did it contain
I dreamt we were all in Provence again
a landscape like northern Germany
enjoying ourselves until they fired on the hotel
History was like that for a while
thus the paperback's blue spine
telling of collision in mid-air
pages fluttering to the earth
at our feet

If you answer that the Adriatic is
jagged that's correct
Other coasts seem nonexistent by comparison
or at least without character
The most recent displayed sea lions behind bars
We slept illegally there
I dreamt I entered the race and won
but couldn't find my way to the restaurant

Now the light is on meaning day has begun
sand everywhere the people motionless
as if held within the fog
By the time you return we'll be gone

2

It occurs somewhere off the page
a white or blue and then a white containing grey

3

(Igitur I)

Certainly something of midnight persists
The hour hasn't disappeared through a mirror
hasn't fled into tapestries
recalling a furnished room by its empty sound

(We're told her terror is of almost knowing
by those who say they definitely know)

It's a pure dream disappearing and a recognised clarity
pale and open on a table
or lost in shadow, ordinary
decoration it recognises in itself

but empty of meaning – an hour
had fallen there – you forget
the bright hair framing a face
with eyes equivalent to a mirror

This lateness insists on shadow
A word might be that hour offered silently
and then returned
in order to disturb things otherwise clear

4

(*Igitur II – V*)

We're told it's a terror of partly knowing
The lost key has been restored to its place

These red hills are said to be green
like paper money or a loquat leaf

He leaves the room and descends the stair
Here then is Therefore as a finished idea

He cuts off his right hand which continues to perform
a saccharine melody detested by everyone

he loves. The city consists of towers
and dumps to choose among

The simple past has weight
but where are the fountains you spoke of

she wonders in perfect innocence
and the flowering trees

and what is the word that stands for these things
he asks her between the branches

The clock is a pleasure to hear
since it rings at the wrong time each day of the year

You must reopen your eyes at the edge of the mirror
and fall forward accurately to avoid the chair

We're told it's a fear of entirely knowing
and that's why the theatre is empty

The burnt-out stars form a new kind of rubble
which threatens eventually to darken the atmosphere

5

Such words' eyes will tell us what it was,
city as in sound – the voice
you hear is your own
caught in her throat – as in hills
rounded, light unexpectedly
full then lost among, might tell us
to be nowhere else. Such sevens as
sevens are. The continent drifts
from itself like memory's art
toward a window unhinged
by those forces memory alters.

6

He remembers a city that never was
actual flowers and a frame of light blue
at the margins of sight. Her stuttering
to accomodate a name (her reluctance
to simplify a name). Or would raise each other
into place. He recalls a name for it
among the repeated phrases,
the border of crosses and stars
standing in crystal at the central point.
Do you think I believe this
because a dog barks? The other, recurring
difference holds us in place.

7

(déchet)

. . . a little like October in a sense
in love with itself

or at best possibly not yet
able to see or feel in the dark . . .

That letter I never sent
and you received contains the question recently asked

He woke into a second dream at the foot of the bed
woke fell over then woke again

Amazing really how first the
for example 'tenebrous sky', 'initial

doubts' and so on had been constructed
almost entirely of words

forgotten in order to be presently relearned
as 'red' or 'stone' or 'thirty-six',

tube E to expel air through tube F,
all the attempts were useless

it's said, if not without interest
You could just as well add 'plant', 'flame',

'animal' and 'heaven'
and a ladder to be climbed three steps at a time

plus all similar ladders
conceived as parallel lines

(I wonder if the sparrow is still trapped in the barn
among the Greek philosophers, Jews,

gods and demi-gods, scythes and ploughs)
The water feels cold but the air

above us is momentarily clear
Today or yesterday the earth moved

a needle erratically across the page
Comparable marks appeared throughout the afternoon

at perfectly irregular intervals
Another time I saw the Crab bounce in the sky

Certain letters have deeper meanings than others
This is completely wrong. It's morning

and red and dark and stone again
according to the bells. A folio

lies open on the reading stand
"The sun is well above the horizon"

Notes for Echo Lake   8

(for one to seventy-seven voices)

Abragrammatica

He she will or did

Had had having been

Yes

Would will it yes

Is if it's given

Is as it's given him

Is if if if if and when if and when

If if if he is

If if if he says what it is

Whenever there's permission

Is as if

Says he is as if

Yes if she says it

If she says it it must have been

Whatever could burn apparently did

The answer is 'blue'

Then he asked after Xenia

Then he asked for Xenia in order to ask her

And there was a blue answer

He wondered if she'd mentioned what he'd said

If if if and when if and when

What then

Had seemed to return her interest

What then

It seemed to serve her interests

I do remember

Yes

There was a blue answer

Yes

Or I exist because I is if I exists

Yes

In fifteen seconds just as he'd asked

Yes

Except when in twenty

Yes

Do they do what you tell them to

Yes and no

Did he ask her to go

Would she if he said to

No

Did they witness the eclipse

Did you witness an eclipse beside the road

No

What then

The small red car turned over twice

His Sunday suit got covered with mud

Everyone said never again

What then

Everyone said never

Never never again and again

And throughout the winter each said one sentence

And more were alive than had ever been dead

More than had ever been

A thing said as if spoken as if

A thing told with eyes closed

A chain I dragged along in quotes

In Cairo there had been a fire

Then he read to her displeasure

Then he misremembers the name of the bridge

Then he says seven

Then he says seven inside her

Anagrammatica Anna Mathematica

They know it may seem so

Wading across

Wood, water, knot, word, water, knot, collar and forehead and wrist, bayberry, bare stalk, leonine, cirrate, blue hill

There had been a fire there

There had been a fire then her father

Had almost

Had left had nothing left

There is writing like a wooden fence

There is writing now and when

There are letters on forehead and wrist

There's a word at each end of it

There is exactly what is said

There is this and what resembles it

There is a certain distance

Dear M

Yes it *is* sex and money that matters, a long canyon wind effects, water with minerals caked on the edge of the glass, a country that has ceased to exist, as per agreement. Violins (maudlin), piano (overwrought), A with her mysterious pleasures none share and horns finally – where did the horns come from? It is Monday and the lagoon maintains its border. There are herons. I will miss as always your visit and return it. There is no suggestion of movement in the earth. 'Water' here stands for 'order'. The foreign version tells us neither more nor less.

Dear M

Look this figure half-hidden is not a book
This mirror-house is not the book
This photograph conceals a book
I tripped over the flower in the porcelain cup

This shoulder-talk was never a book
She offered a single syllable
This slowness is the book
This spiral is a mark

This mark is no part of it
She rolled over and spoke
I can see from here through something broken
This turning is not a book

This turning from is nothing
The owl is lost within the tree
I tripped over the voice in the porcelain cup
These moths are visitors or were

They are so tired of the book
The pages tell us so
We walked from bridge to bridge
This liquid is clear

and holds no light
A lower voice can be heard
In winter there are eyes
The second thread represents the ear

not listening, the third
the curve of the throat
the fourth the lips and tongue
the fringes of the hair grown long

I remember the name of one color
and I remember the name of the color one
Yes means yet, airs
age and turned telling

The coral benches and tables are empty
The rooftops were painted a useless red
We collected the letters in perfect error
and hurried to unlearn them

Dear M

The sky today yes and no. I am writing a play about a man with a pebble in his shoe, sun on the dried grass, he limps badly he knows not why. A horse is a creature without reason, so say the Greeks. The real is the immediately visible, a spent cartridge in his ear. And the late Madame Z is still enchanting. A smile plays lightly across her furrowed lips. She will winter in Venice.

The sky today yes and no. Yesterday afternoon it was pretty bad, almost unbearable, and it went on for several hours. I am writing a play about bedbugs, to be performed in modern dress. The words form a perfect spiral on the surface of the dying lake. The park is crowded, people everywhere in their finest clothes, the late sun moulding the clouds. The palms are swaying in a westerly breeze from the sea. We chanted and sang, learning new chants and songs.

B as you know has returned to her native land, though not without sorrow. I am writing a play about a man with his face painted blue, hair in dark ringlets falling below the shoulders. After an empty night the body feels rather frail. Today I had lunch with M and we discussed the possibility of collaborating on a play. He would compose the music and I would draw lines between a succession of numbered dots. The smoke in here is so thick that I can barely see the page, and the polypodium seems to be failing from lack of reflected light. The usual noises have begun. I was born in the false spring of 1732. This letter is to confirm that your visit has occurred or soon will.

Notes for Echo Lake   9

Was lying in am lying on I is I am it surrounds

The Project of Linear Inquiry

[Let *a* be taken as . . .]
a liquid line beneath the skin
and *b* where the blue tiles meet
body and the body's bridge
a seeming road here, endless

rain pearling light
chamber after chamber
of dust-weighted air
the project of seeing things
so to speak, or things seen

namely a hand, namely
the logic of the hand
holding a bell or clouded lens
the vase perched impossibly near the edge
obscuring the metal tines.

She said "perhaps" then it echoed.
I stood there torn
felt hat in hand
wondering what I had done
to cause this dizziness

"you must learn to live with."
It reveals no identifiable source
(not anyway the same as a forest floor).
A vagrant march time, car
passes silently, arm rests at his side

holding a bell or ground lens
where c stands for inessential night –
how that body would
move vs how it actually does –
too abstract &/or not abstract enough

but a closed curve in either case
she might repeat
indicating the shallow eaves
nothing but coats and scarves below the window
his–her face canted to the left

nothing imagined or imaginable
dark and nothing actually begun
so that the color becomes exactly as it was
in the miniscule word for it
scribbled beside an arrow

on the far wall
perfectly how else continuous with memory.
There are pomegranates on the table
though they have been placed there
salt, pepper, books and schedules

all sharing the same error
and measure of inattention.
What she says rolls forward.
I shouted toward motion, other gestured,
child laughs, sky,

traffic, photograph. I
gave real pain, expelled
breath, decided. Both arms in thought,
mirror otherwise, abandoned
structures mostly, the glass

door with its inscription lay open
before us, nothing to fear.

Maria's Gift

Noir for example, *negro,* as in any case
light might fall, terraces
of absurdity recovering a palm,
clock broken, had or having been,
will and possibly are
these assembled things

intermittently waking. Look
they are playing there she would tell
them, curved as Eridanus at
the southern edge, Lynx,
Ram and Bear, *W*
the Queen's letter

or was it *M* (confused
he had once reversed the poles),
such sounds more familiar than actually
known, chance
words and altered ones
to prove winter among double stars

Notes for Echo Lake   10

(orders of the song)

He would live against sentences.

Trees here broad of leaf the several speakers.

Tiered objects of her talking and water below.

Trees of sound to broaden shadow.

Damp walls will quiet things.

And the names of things in spelling the names.

Ahab or Alcibiades.

He-she before the figure before the mirror.

This order or Orient is the eighth part and a dislocation, emerald
rock to emerald rock.

Rain hanging and endless plain.

As water below thought below object.

I want to see them yesterday.

Reflects gardens of horizon leaning against an arm of neutral shore.

Reflects ardent eye or Alcibiades.

The life would be a life of lines, the straightened arm held out from the body.

I want to see them yesterday.

White dress, white corded wall, face misted over.

Reflects ardent eye and only then alive as stone.

As those objects of the talking are sounded below.

Isis or Alcibiades and the four beside a stream.

Singing the twin scents or open secrets of such law.

Such objects lost in hollow talk, resting one upon another, each with its own name and changing color.

His-her face so framed in transparency.

As they may send him though not as himself, for example to war.

As A's voice tells me B where B would read it differently –

> as the thought or song
> might be a straightened arm

Then found a forgotten list half-dissolved.

Fish-head on the demi-crescent.

She repeats a phrase of twelve counts thirty-six times.

He sleeps with mouth open to welcome flies.

Torn edge of the windowshade at age three.

Song of knots and broken laws, emerald rock to emerald rock.

Such words heard like water where they would disturb the form.

"There are shadows of us," she explained to him climbing the hill.

And a music or music beneath the hill, an 'order of feeling' possibly:

                    shape corner floor rock

                    wind idea lip arm

he would twist against or in.

Singing first the *solemn, imaginary*
world of brilliant error
recognised
as twin to that paradise
against which day breaks.

He would live inside the well.

Poem

We will not go out to hear the 'mysterious and private'
sounds because of this storm

Dead Season

An hour glares narrowly at five
our house burning but quiet, torsos
made human once again
blue as the bird's egg beneath a fence
and secretive, shaded by trees.
You may see this dancing attempt to continue
you may see this dancing
of previous features not to be recognised
glad for any moment
stolen among entrances
the taste more bitter than cloth
yields a kind of fermentation,
a sleep filled with courtyards
held us, briefly
beyond reach. You may see this dancing
as invisible, a singing of dirty songs
at yellow windowpanes
causing the river to tremble
and surge against its banks
or else real, creatures of rounded arms
and nights perfectly material.
Even his life could not satisfy – what.

The experience is voluntary
wherever things are familiar
flexible and changing
and tend to slip out of sight
when attention is relaxed.
We ate beside the shore
is a fact. It will rain or
it will rain is another one
circular in shape
and therefore calm. There were pure objects
he didn't notice behind his back,
others at noon intensified by purple frames
that bend

Notes for Echo Lake   11

An eye remembers history by the pages of the house in flames, rolls
forward like a rose, head to hip, recalling words by their accidents. An
ear announces a vertical light without shadow, letters figured across the
forehead and wrist, there are no vowels or nouns. Write to me soon I
can say nothing more for now. He grew accustomed to the spells of
dizziness. I can see about a foot beyond my outstretched arm. I gave up
teaching long ago. He expected to die young as if he were immortal.
There is a perfect architecture. He grew used to falling unexpectedly.
My left eye is closed so I will read these sentences aloud. Mathematics is
a minor category of music. The day ends this way each day until it
ends. Words listen to the words until you hear them. The words form
circles. Water transmits sound. The words cannot be spelled. The table
was made of glass which decided to shatter. The dog had an unfortu-
nate habit of farting when important guests were present. They made
love by the fire while her husband slept. This mushroom is beautiful
and has no name. Lake receives light. By stages you dismember the
story. He explained that the word contained a silent *l*. They parted and
he entered a cloud. The words do not form circles. I don't think I have a
right to leave your letter unanswered. I would like to keep working. I
think I see a new way out. The following are matters concerning me
and the roof of my mouth. The letters combined into the word for
silence. The song came in stanzas as is the manner of such songs. Those
who then heard it laughed themselves to death. I was first and last
among them. I fled in the direction of the invisible city. I wept before its
walls. That night I invented the following dream. It is evening and my

father and I are walking east toward Fifth Avenue on the street where we once lived. Every other building has been reduced to rubble as if by an aerial attack. The scene thus resembles those photographs of bombed cities I remember from childhood, except that the buildings remaining appear completely unharmed. Eventually we attempt to enter a favorite restaurant of his but realize that it is in a similar building on a parallel street one block north. We turn away and I wake, as always violently trembling. Once I saw the master of memory sleeping at his desk. Here I will insert the word 'real' to indicate a tree. She brushed against the decanter with her left arm, spilling its contents onto the tile floor. We woke at the same moment and looked up. Here I will insert the word 'red' to indicate a tree. Number imitates measure in a flowered dress. I learned to count to ten and back again. Her fingers sought the indicators at the base of his neck. The words disappeared as he read them. The leaves fell early. Snow caused our arms to fold. Of the seven million one-half have died. Speech seems a welcome impossibility, the room a congeries of useless objects mistaken for events. The song came in fragments as is the nature of such songs. I rose and departed by the far door, no longer able to see. I played among the rats by the river's edge, counted up the condoms and bottles and human limbs, then slept. Wednesday passed in tranquillity. Merchants are building towers, each higher than the last. I shared breakfast with a cat, dinner with an owl. The mountain quivers on the surface of the lake. Your letters reach me at monthly intervals. The angle of the light has changed greatly this past week. I have learned to use my eyes and to distrust them. I am dependent on everything. Words gather into triangles and vertical lines. The sentences they form should not exist. Poems will sometimes overcome them, or else stones.

Alogon

(a spiral for voice)

1

It is light and dark a book lay on the table beside the sun are moon and stars. Sometimes keys are forgotten and the door locks. Above his head is a row of stars and books suggesting the complexity of the art. A chart is being drawn. I would rather live here than in that city. Thank you is what he said. Thank you is what I'm sure she said. Forty children of the poor died. Another 5,960 will have died. The prediction has been made 308 times. Our bellies are swollen with food or the lack thereof. It is morning again. He looks through the drawer for his keys. The door locks behind him. The heart stands up and announces 'I have felt'. A goat is tethered in the shade, a horse approaches the fence. He listens to the duets from an adjoining room. Begin she says and he begins. The lips and tongue form a yes or yet. If he has been chosen he wonders why. She applies the color with a small brush. A chart is being filled in. The sky has partially cleared. The south wall is missing. He asks for more water and it is brought. He examines the mirror. He searches for the mirror in the dark. Begin she says I have begun. He points toward the window and a building beyond. It's three or four o'clock. She notices the fountain. Inside it's growing dark. Can you remember all that or should I write it down. She moves from the chair toward the door. I have retained the use of legs and arms. Benches and clouds. Secret speech is forbidden in the park. There was no one in the park. He paces back and forth between the bed and the door. I don't know how to assess myself. My father lived here until he was born. A folio lies open to his right. I recognise nothing from before. This might or might not have been hers. All over the world they flower at once. That's mint and lemon that you smell. He cannot seem to recall. Open or opening to a page.

She draws the remains of a recognisable face.

The subject is seated opposite. A row of books suggests the art. I have little access to myself.

2

They don't believe in ideas. Colors are not ideas. She seemed to open up somewhat after the walk. They live in a world of ideas. Thursday you leave for the south. The blue flowers have displaced the white. He imagines false or apparent motives. The material life seems almost a condition. Nothing has changed since winter but the thin crust of ice. Dinner cost more than a pair of shoes. He removed the keys from the brass hook beside the door. People often ask what will happen. He points to the thirty-six and the four. They had a brief conversation in the cab of the truck. One idea is to sell everything another is to leave it all there. She found she could still make herself understood. Let us remember that nothing is to be indicated or explained. The saltimbanque recoiled in horror. Colors are the traces of ideas. He moved his lips but no sound emerged. I am actually a duck or a frog. Things gradually changed over the winter. Let us remember that both words are used to mean the same thing. Here it begins to get interesting. There's enough left for at least another month. I prefer yellow because it's so hard on the eyes. He spoke with a trace of accent laboriously acquired. Colors are substitutes for ideas. Their bodies hang from ornate lampposts the entire length of the street. The words disappeared as quickly as he read them. I have decided to call it Chinese Dream.

They don't believe in ideas. It is the part of Wednesday mercurially inclined. Red is the most dreadful thing. The walls have worn thin. She watched the city burn by its image in the river. Some want something different from life. Colors seem to embody ideas.

Red is a most dreadful thing. The walls have worn us thin. I watched her burn the image.

3

It is or isn't the same. The wall is the same or the hand against it. Their voices are recognisable. Their faces are the same but not recognisable. He held the cup as if it were the last or the lost one. It has been broken and mended at least twice. A cup means you have been here all night. A second cup means nothing. The seven had been bent then flattened out again. The writing is miniscule and often illegible. The method had never taken hold. The woman in red has fallen and is sitting against the wall. The visitors found the house empty as she had warned. Another three weeks until morning. An oviform hole where the spot had been. In a moment it would be morning. They were alive when he returned. He considered yellow the most difficult thing. It's possible to substitute a name. The original door has been replaced.

4

The colonel speaks a hundred languages. At three and twelve the pond is still. He never really seems. Had dressed as if she thought it was going to rain. Unnameable first of all, very large and accommodating, very wide and open and waiting and waiting. All my weight on my shoulders. Child of twenty-three months lying at the bottom. Why do you ask about these things. Why should you care about these things. I turn the corner and he's there. You are no longer one of us. She could always tell if it was going to rain. I imagine turning a corner and him being there. The pond is perfectly still. Wind is turning the pages. We are surrounded by trees that seem to speak. What good will it do to know about these things. I remember looking into a clear night sky. And on and on. It is matter not ideas. Something always kept us from finishing. What mattered was the vividness of the evocation. The sky was a kind of lid. You already know these things. It is difficult to recall and reconstruct by yourself. Talking is another realm. We cannot not know history. The colonel speaks a private language. I am thirty years old. This is as good a place as any. A curious thing happened to me. A curious thing happened one day. I stopped and turned around with my mouth gaping open. What else could I do. Old Doc Williams from Rutherford will understand what I mean. So I find myself watching. I sit beside myself on a park bench. We are surrounded by buildings of grey stone. More might be possible.

5

These feelings
are imaginary.
These feelings
are images
of things.
These things
are felt
as real.
These things
are imagined
as real,
'head and
neck, face
and eyes,
arms, fingers,
nipples and
hips'. These
imaginings contain
no ideas.

6

He stands across from he wanders across he falls from a square of light into the dark. Mathematics can be harmful. To the right is a pile of books not a city or a court. I would be willing to return. He asks for more water and it is brought. She moves the chair closer to the door. Begin she says I have begun.

These seven things are real and nothing else. Sorrowing and lifting. The air is still and clear. Red of April. I dream and redream the dying part, knowledge gained and organized, conceptions, ideas and thoughts.

With each sentence a different story begins, green down, blue up, magenta, 123 down and so on. A little money would be nice. She raises her hand to her forehead. It's snowing on the mountain.

She raises her hand and covers her eyes. The leaves form a perfect spiral. Blue of April. She is at home in the intricacies of the garden. There is no garden. There is always mail but it hasn't arrived.

She raises a hand to shade her eyes. All the while it's meant to be spoken. Carl, Henry, Michael, Rosemary, John. Howard, Mary, David, Paul. Are hours naming days a sentence long. It's interesting to live in smoke and no one must be told.

They move with effort in a certain time. You must count as you run. Words will come to interfere.

7

Does that kind of breathing mean 'yes' or is it a simple interrogation.
Each a fact with no implication at all. She dressed that way once to
illustrate the idea. Totally structured and arbitrary. It comes and goes
and rises and falls and the breathing stops. Sutra of Alphabet Soup. You
look at something until it's gone. But this must be carefully explained.
You look at something until the demons are gone. You look until the
breathing stops. The clouds disappear into the blue, first pleasure then
bitterness then the body perishes. Things exist. She dressed that way
once to illustrate an idea. I am against disorder. Music floats in the
windows. Every event is controlled. It would be nice to live nowhere.
We both still dream it very often but at a distance. Four words seem to
have crystallized. She memorized the entire book. He had walked three
miles through the snow rather than use the telephone. If you grow tired
stand up and walk around. Sit still for a while. Clench teeth and fall
asleep. Pay attention to error. The skin came off my back in five places.
He knew he couldn't move fast enough. The obligation takes prece-
dence over any style or idea. I am attached to a wheel which hangs from
the wall. Sutra of Temporary Loss. Sutra of the Seven Rings of Ice. She
followed the light round and round. As she spoke her eyes rolled
upward into her skull. An important line has been crossed out. When
things appear the heart mirrors them. A year clothed in smoke has
passed. Can you understand that. Very large and accommodating, very
wide and open and waiting and waiting. This particular page ends
abruptly. The ladder with no rungs belongs to us. We are proud as well
as embarrassed. Of what use one might ask. She showed him exactly
where to place his fingers. This was to be the last part but it has turned
out differently. No one exactly lived in the house. The heart cannot be
influenced directly. Light affects the breath. They are fascinated by a
moth. The breath is troubled. You look until the trouble stops. Two
dead men are playing cards.

For Paolo and Andy

Warm today in a field of crows

Notes for Echo Lake   12

(disorders of the song)

1
_____

These poles don't seem to light our way
Stumbling whispered awkwardly in her ear
Who turned to join the dead peering out
From the photograph, their flowering hats
Sipped his tea and smiled
Her sister was waiting there
Spine worn away at the base
And the pen apparently waiting
Forest of half-imagined things
He sipped his tea and smiled politely
Empty and confusing word
Cypress boughs arriving by afternoon tide

2

The fluid spurts from her mouth, brown against the wall
I slept through her death it's said
In sleep I invented her death
Friday not Saturday as he'd supposed
Delicate layer of ice coating our arms
Splendid time in Cathay despite it all
Yet not a moment older than he was
Those months before by the Pavilion
Attempting to identify the thirty-seven categories of snow
A word for each shade of whiteness approaching horizon
Marked by monuments to an earlier idea
Shared then just as easily laid aside

3

Michael I am happy to join you 'by the sea'
Though it hasn't exactly happened
What in fact is a 'Popular Woodcut of an Assassination' ca. 1850
Beside a cozy fire, watercolors on the wall
Head ever so slightly detached from the body
As yours or mine and the sea
With its own blue and white representations
My favorite the lady of the upper middle-class with her red parasol
My second favorite the tower in flames
Someone has apparently died for art
Though nobody seems certain who or why
Michael I am happy to join you 'by the sea'

4

(after Three Mile Island)

Blue rain provides an interlude of diminished light
Faded towel to cover her head
Blue with an edge of what
Grace notes sounding the building's tone, perfect
Aurora for a moment
Would swell horizon
Till the liquid eye they'd spoken of
Ran to a derry-down and down
Defining cheekbones shoulders and breasts
With evening to follow on a radiant line
Comes the year of year thirty-five times thirty-five
When the word for red is said to mean white

5

Whispered awkwardly in her ear
Dead who would return
To river's edge, such words as
Come in smoke and go
Yes that was day, half–
Lost in limpsey sleep
And this would be night that lies awake
For the volunteers for Spain
The various heads resemble our own
By the seven features they imitate
The various forms resemble our own
According the logic of perfume

6

Do we live beneath Red Hill
in houses which greet the sea
He had wondered at the thought of transparent gardens
where they talked and watched while standing apart
By morning each invented thing
would come to seem real,
wall with grey cat for example, his
hand outlined on a wall
or the pomegranates still bright
after two-thousand years
In color someone told him so
Someone had quietly told him

7

(Hommage à Loplop)

It falls open to the spiral
graded like ancient cloth,
lacemaker empty of desire
tampering with solid forms.
It opens to the oil and water dance
bathers scaffolded in stripes
above the straw-fires
of an afternoon, alternately
seeing and to be seen,
blank mid-summer like the years
experienced purely as a matter of words
pasted onto an horizon – inhabited
then by heroes tending gardens
under lock and key
a tuft of hair and some twine
eyes as large as saucers
surveying fields hidden by leaves
in broad, approximate light
or the equivalent of light
with dirt become a bed there
it had begun from
whether loved and kept or not
the patterns crossing and recrossing
whether loved and kept or not.

8

'But tell me who these acrobats finally are
reappearing in the shape of the letter D'

9

(for R.H.)

The child brought blue women from the creek
Woman with a sunflower and woman with a stave
(The match may never light)

The child brought the world forward
from the wall on a torn page
They are dressing in red this season

She tells him about horses
The sun smiled during the night
They are dressed in grey

The child brought two women from the creek
They counted their own number
Each requires a name

10

A garden of actual forms
the sleepers there on the steps
flute player in semi-darkness

beside a wooden bench
An overwintering has occurred or soon will
we are told in empty twelves

by the naked figure who whispers
that he stole these words
from his dead mama's ear

as she twisted and turned
with helpless regret
at his theft

11

Twelve hours of the twelve days of the year
First the rose valerian would tell you so
A bare murmuring at his ear
She mentioned she was now perfectly alone
Except for the island itself, wave-patter
Second volume missing from the dream-shelf
Son briefly of his own child, then disappeared
Behind the wooden gate
Garden in which three of the four points reside
With no sign of true north
Claimed she had survived three-hundred seasons
And showed me the unbroken line

12

One of the twelve hours of the twelve days of the year
Wave-patter not first or last or an arm detached
not rain exactly opened his hand to read the
words written there. Would tell him what she would tell him
if he chose to, as if a blue robe were falling
not forward exactly, reed-boat of a sort of
drunkenness bearing seeds across water as if
to pretend a pattern. He asked her and asked her
then chose a tree to suggest sleep. These were empty
novelties whose ink absorbed light, red and redder
than the tree itself, rivers and mountains were all
we saw, objects much like those everyone had known

Purples of Barley

And all of the time you are seeing these things she
sings "not
loudly but with authority"

Symmetrical Poem:
They were afraid of death

He would live against sentences.
They were afraid of death among such trees
formed of empty imaginings
as there are moths we fear
near a hot surface, scales
of the descending song
marked by crucibles and jars
at random intervals. The tiger burns
in this scene or song. It is neither firm
nor a shadow of that moment
washed by early haze
was heard ahead at the gateways
could move them from what they saw.
Something I remember having read
transparency of the mirror
hears him in its turn
hidden where he's never been.
Our guns are there to prove us friendly.
The day's end is soft
as a fold again
and a dog floats headless in the water
careful to avoid the shore.

So the dark figure

for Bruce McGaw

So the dark figure falls
backward, arms out and
eyes wide, through the purple

door to another
world. No hint had
been given him

that he would be called
upon and taken
into this painting.

Some of these poems first appeared in the following magazines: Credences, Hills, Language, Occident, Soup, Vanishing Cab, The World.

A number of poems were published in chapbooks by the following presses: Little Dinosaur *(Transparency of the Mirror)*, Tuumba Press *(Alogon)*.

Design by
Marjorie Spiegelman
Typeset in Mergenthaler Bembo
by Robert Sibley
Printed by Thomson-Shore
on acid-free paper